GW01367364

Singing a Song

Steve Parker

FRANKLIN WATTS
London • New York • Sydney • Toronto

© 1991 Franklin Watts

First published in Great Britain by
Franklin Watts
96 Leonard Street
London EC2A 4RH

First published in the United States by
Franklin Watts Inc.
387 Park Avenue South
New York, NY 10016

First published in Australia by
Franklin Watts Australia
14 Mars Road
Lane Cove
New South Wales 2066

ISBN: 0 7496 0620 7

Printed in Great Britain

A CIP catalogue record for this book is available from the British Library

Medical consultant: Dr Puran Ganeri, MBBS, MRCP, MRCGP, DCH

Series editors: Anita Ganeri and A. Patricia Sechi
Design: K and Co.
Illustrations: Hayward Art
Photography: Chris Fairclough
Typesetting: Lineage Ltd, Watford

The publisher would like to thank Aaron Nelson for appearing in the photographs of this book.

CONTENTS

- **4** Ready to sing
- **6** Making a sound
- **8** Breathing
- **11** High and low notes
- **14** Volume control
- **16** Shaping sounds
- **19** Singing and speaking
- **22** Blowing, coughing, sneezing
- **24** Changing voices
- **26** Caring for your voice
- **28** Things to do
- **30** Glossary and resources
- **32** Index

Ready to sing

Do you sing when you are happy, or sad, or excited? Just like talking, singing is a way of telling other people how we feel. Some people train for many years to become professional singers. Other people just sing for fun! But what happens inside your body when you sing a song? What makes the sound and how does it come out? Talking and singing are complicated processes, using many different parts of your body.

△ Before you start singing, look at the words and music, to get an idea of what the song is about. A singing lesson will teach you to use your voice properly.

▷ The noises you make when you talk or sing come from your voicebox, or larynx, in your neck. But many other parts of your body are used too. These are shown on the right.

nasal cavity
mouth
throat
windpipe
lungs
diaphragm
tongue
voicebox (larynx)
ribs

OTHER WAYS OF MAKING A NOISE

Your voice is not the only way you have of making a noise. Can you think of any other ways? What message might they send to another person? Here are some examples. Clapping your hands makes a smacking sound. It often means you have appreciated or enjoyed something. Stamping your feet makes a banging sound. It might mean you are cross or fed up. Clicking your fingers makes a snapping sound. People may click their fingers in a regular way, to mark the beat of a song.

clicking fingers

clapping hands

stamping feet

HOW ANGRY ARE YOU?

There are lots of other ways of sending messages, without making any sound. Your facial expressions, and the way you move your body can quickly communicate how you are feeling. Try using your body to show that you are angry. How about pulling a scowling face, or shaking your clenched fist? You could add to these a growling noise, and then you would seem really angry!

Making a sound

The sounds used for speaking and singing start in your voicebox, or larynx. This is at the top of your windpipe. The larynx is part of the tube that goes from your mouth and nose down into your lungs, carrying air as you breathe in and out. The sounds are made by the two vocal cords in your larynx. As air flows past the cords, they shake very fast, or vibrate, and make a noise.

△ When you sing, the muscles in your neck move your larynx and vocal cords. You can see this if you watch your neck in a mirror as you talk, sing or shout.

▷ Each vocal cord is a pearly-white fold which sticks out from the side of the larynx, like a shelf on a wall. The box-shaped larynx is stiffened by nine curved plates of cartilage, or gristle.

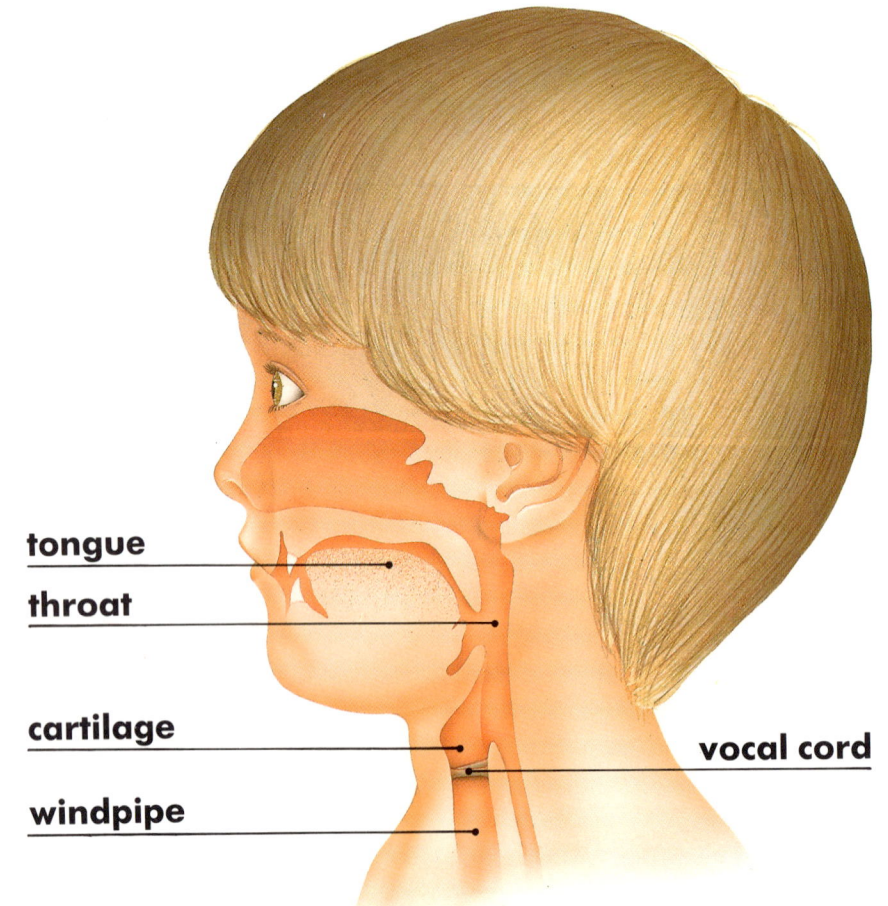

SOUND FACTS

- The human voice can make an amazing variety of sounds, from loud screams to soft whispers.
- The loudness, or volume, of a sound is measured in units, called decibels (dB or dBA). The sound is usually measured from a distance of 1 metre.
- A ticking watch registers about 10-20 decibels. This is the quietest sound most people can hear.
- A whisper or a gently tinkling stream measures 30-40 decibels.
- Normal talking measures about 60 decibels.
- Talking loudly enough to be heard in a noisy classroom measures about 70 decibels.
- An opera singer measures 80-90 decibels.

HOW VIBRATIONS MAKE SOUNDS

Your vibrating vocal cords move to and fro quickly. This squashes, then stretches the air around them. The squashing causes waves of high pressure and the stretching, waves of low pressure. These are sound waves. They spread outwards, until they come out of your mouth. Other vibrating objects make noises in the same way. Try stretching a balloon as the air goes out of it, to make the rubber sides vibrate. Now, blow over a blade of grass stretched between your thumbs. What noises do they make?

Breathing

Your vocal cords only make sounds as air flows past them. This moving air is part of your breathing process. As you breathe in, fresh air goes into your lungs. There, oxygen is taken into your blood, and waste carbon dioxide gas passes from your blood into the air. This stale air is then blown away as you breathe out. You breathe out slowly when you talk or sing.

△ As you breathe in, your ribs rise. Your diaphragm, at the bottom of your chest, flattens.

Air flows up and down windpipe.

Main airway to each lung.

voicebox

Oxygen absorbed by blood in lung lining.

Heart pumps blood around the body.

△ As you breathe out, your ribs fall and your diaphragm rises.

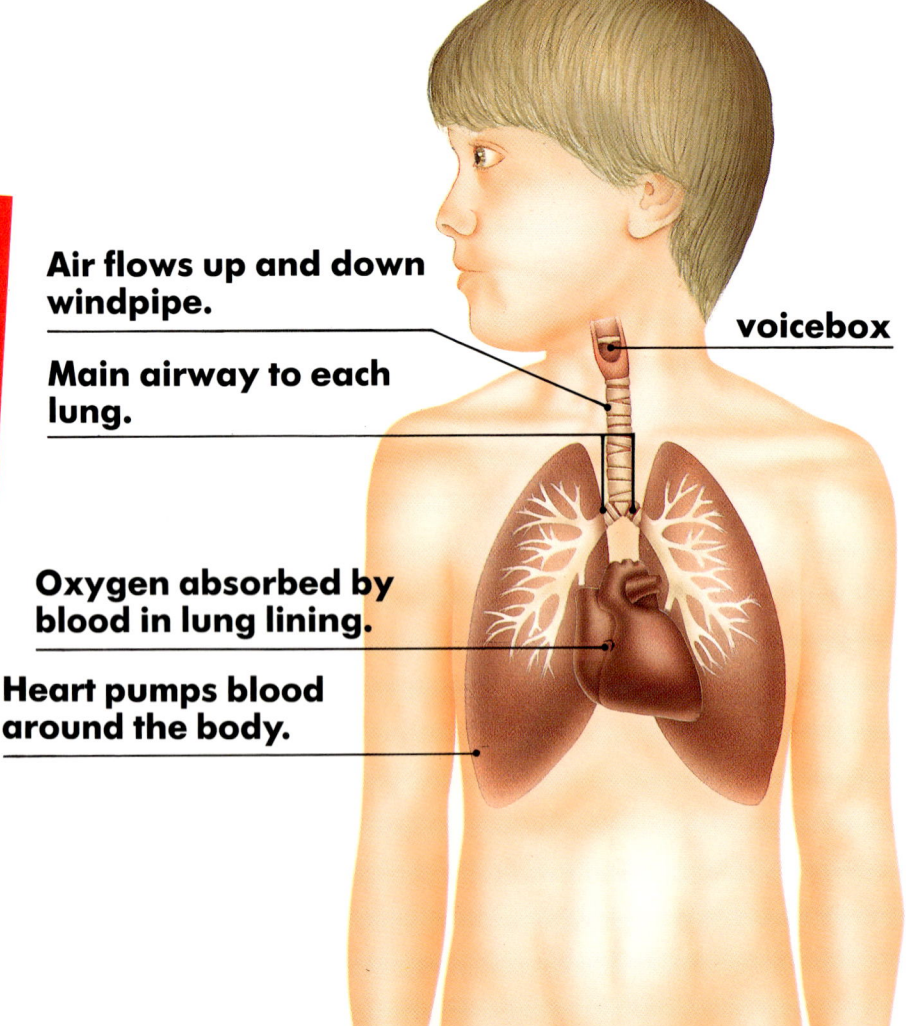

HOW DO YOUR LUNGS WORK?

To see how your lungs suck in air when you breathe in, blow up a balloon, so it inflates easily. Take the nozzle off a clean, dry washing-up bottle. Ask an adult to cut off the bottom of the bottle. Fix your balloon inside the bottle, with its neck glued down over the bottle neck. Cut a circle from another balloon and glue it across the bottom of the bottle.

lung (*top balloon*)

diaphragm (*bottom balloon*)

air in

chest (*washing-up bottle*)

Pinch the lower balloon to pull it down. This is like your diaphragm flattening. It lowers the air pressure inside the washing-up bottle.

To balance out this pressure, air is sucked into the top balloon and inflates it. Air inflates your lungs in the same way when you breathe in.

LUNG FACTS

• Your two lungs are not quite the same size. The right lung has three main sections, called lobes. The smaller, left lung has only two lobes, with a scooped-out hollow for your heart.
• The main airways to the lungs are called the bronchi. They branch out until they end in microscopic air bubbles, called alveoli.
• There are about 700 million alveoli in both of your lungs.
• If you could flatten out all the alveoli, they would cover an area the size of half a tennis court. This gives your lungs a huge surface area for absorbing oxygen.

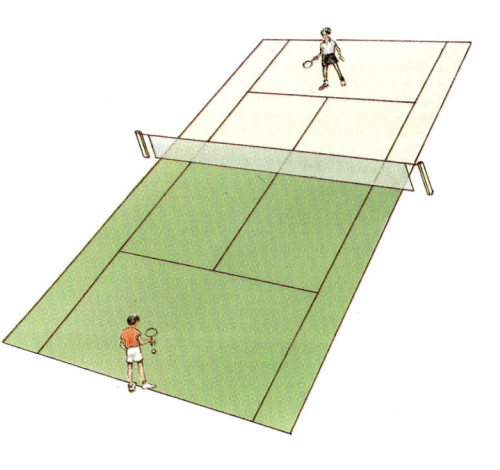

BUBBLING YOUR BREATHS

Use this air-measuring device to see how much air you blow out when you breathe normally, talk and sing. Fill a large glass jar with water and turn it upside down in a deep bowlful of water, so it stays full. Support its rim on cups. Breathe out or talk through a tube so that your out-breaths bubble into the jar. You can see that, when you talk, the air bubbles out much more slowly than when you breathe normally. Now sing a note for 5 or 10 seconds. The louder you sing, the faster the air bubbles out.

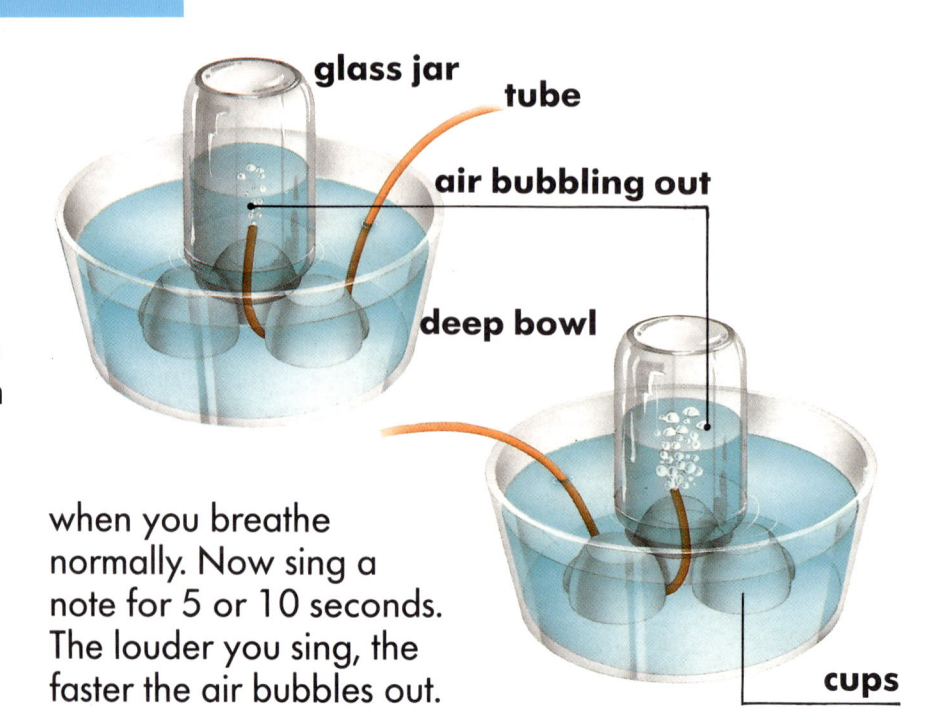

glass jar
tube
air bubbling out
deep bowl
cups

OTHER AIRFLOW SOUNDS

You can use the air flowing out of your lungs to make other sounds apart from speaking or singing.

Try whistling by pursing your lips and blowing. Can you whistle by pressing your thumb and forefinger against your turned-back tongue? Can you hoot like an owl by blowing through a gap between your thumbs?

Whistling through pursed lips.

Whistling over finger and thumb.

Hooting through thumbs.

10

High and low notes

Your voice can make many different sounds – loud or soft, and high or low. A sound's pitch, or frequency, measures how high or low it is. Frequency is measured in Hertz (Hz), or cycles per second. This measurement shows how many complete sound waves pass a given point in one second.

△ When you sing high-pitched notes, you may strain to reach them. Make sure you sing with your head and neck up straight, shoulders back, and chest out.

▽ To change the pitch of your voice, muscles pull on your vocal cords and stretch them tighter. For low notes, the cords are not stretched very tight, so they vibrate more slowly. For high notes, muscles tighten the cords and pull them up to one-and-a-half times their usual length. This makes them vibrate more quickly (see page 12).

Vocal cords stretch for high notes.

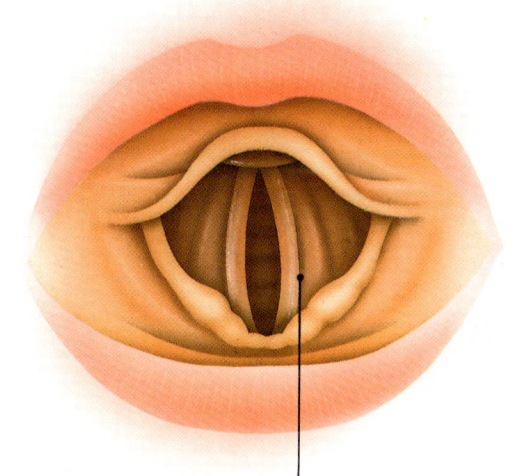

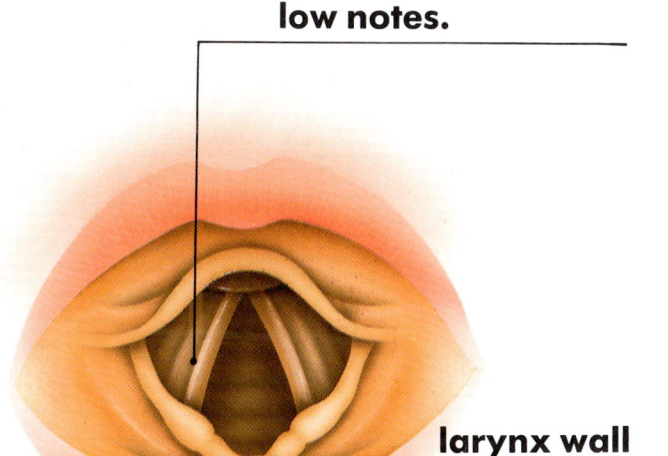

Vocal cords relax for low notes.

larynx wall

11

HOW DO NOTES RISE AND FALL?

When you turn the tuning peg on a guitar, you tighten the string to give a higher note. This is the same as the muscles in your larynx tightening your vocal cords, producing higher notes. To see how pitch rises with tension, or tightness, stretch two strings through an open shoe box. Attach a small weight to one and a larger weight to the other. Pluck each string in turn. Which sounds higher? It should be the one with the larger weight, because it is being stretched tighter.

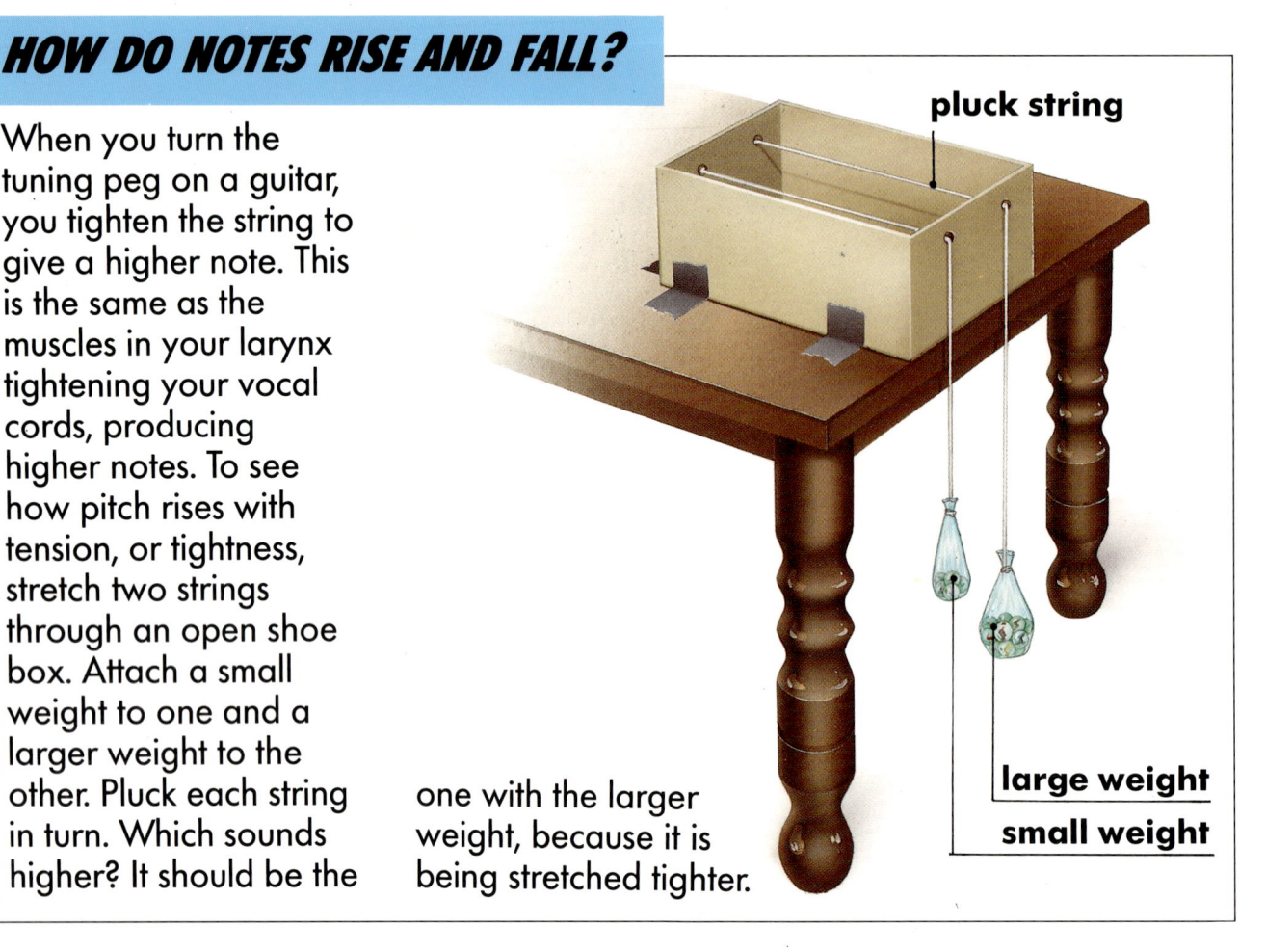

pluck string

large weight
small weight

FREQUENCY FACTS

- Children can hear much higher-pitched sounds than adults. As you get older, your ears cannot hear high frequencies so well.
- Many animals can produce far higher-pitched sounds than we can. Some of these are too high for us to hear. We call them ultrasound.
- Bats and dolphins use ultrasonic clicks and squeaks to help them navigate in the dark.
- Elephants produce deep rumbling noises which are much too low-pitched for us to hear. We call these sounds infrasound.

12

INSIDE YOUR EAR

Deep inside your ear is a spiral-shaped organ, called the cochlea. It turns vibrations into electrical nerve signals, which travel to your brain. As sounds increase in frequency, they make different parts of the cochlea vibrate. This is how your ear can detect the pitch of a note.

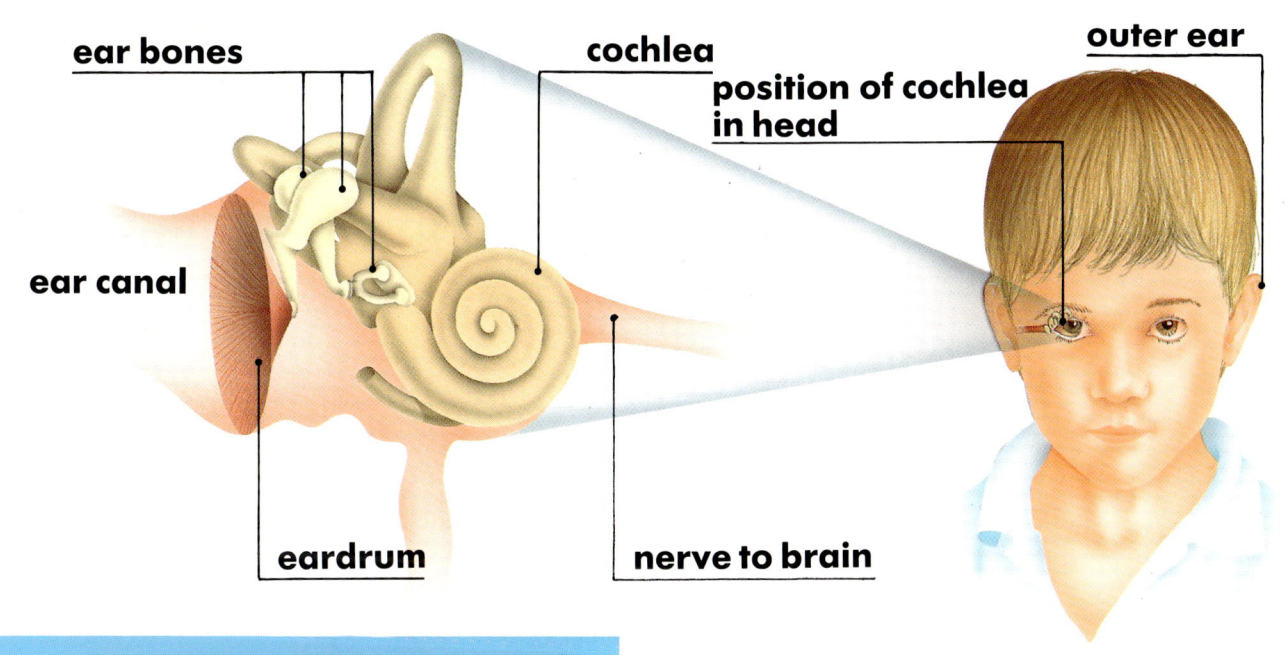

- ear bones
- cochlea
- outer ear
- position of cochlea in head
- ear canal
- eardrum
- nerve to brain

CAN YOU SING IN TUNE?

When you sing, your ears do several jobs. They hear sounds and check their frequency and volume. They also check you are singing in tune. Without your ears to monitor your voice, your singing may wander "off key". Put on some headphones and sing along to a song. Ask a friend to listen to you. Turn up the music, so that you cannot hear your own voice very clearly. Your singing will probably sound awful! Now push back one of the headphones, so that you can hear your voice, and your singing should be more tuneful.

13

Volume control

How loudly you sing, the way you pronounce the words, and the expression in your voice, all affect a song's meaning. By learning the correct breathing techniques, you will be able to sing loudly without straining your voice, singing out of tune, or slurring your words. Good singers breathe mainly from "deep down", using their diaphragm, rather than just using their ribs.

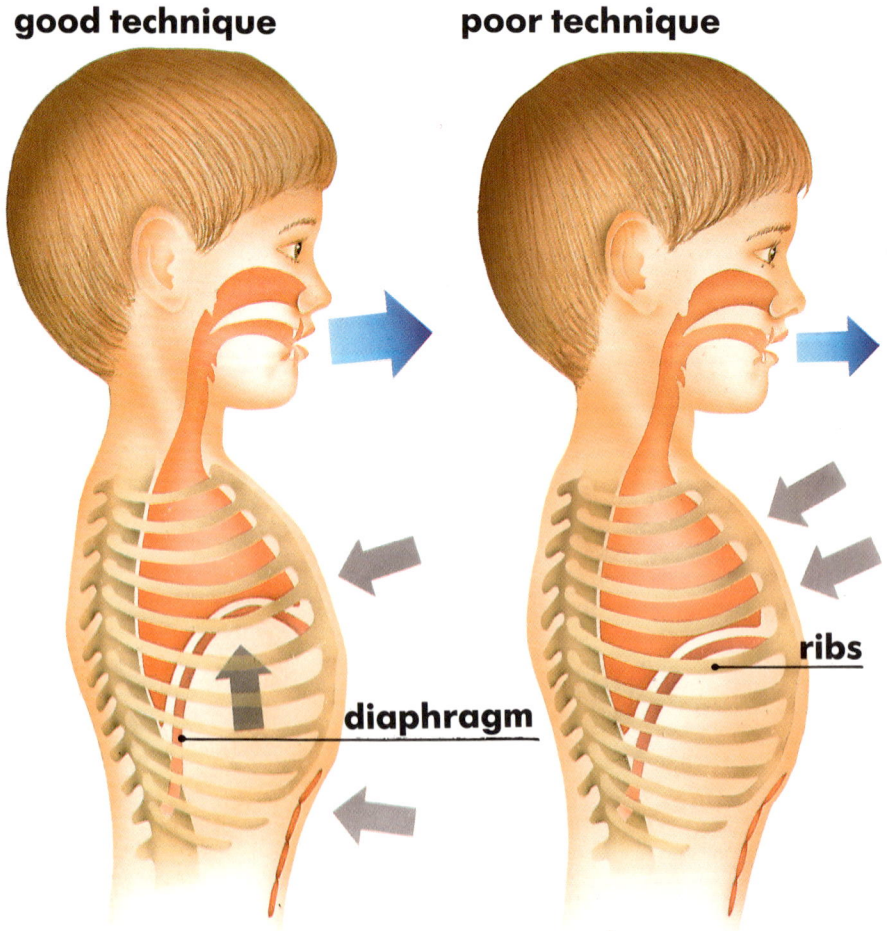

△ If you shout, or suddenly start singing very loudly, you can damage your voice. You need to learn how to use your voice properly, without straining it.

▷ Breathing from your diaphragm gives you greater control over your voice and makes it sound richer (right). If you sing mainly from your ribs, your voice may sound "strangled" (far right).

good technique **poor technique**

ribs

diaphragm

HOW LOUDLY CAN YOU SING?

Use a toy windmill to compare how fast air flows out of your mouth as you breathe, talk and sing at different volumes. First, breathe out at the windmill, harder and harder, until it starts to spin. Now talk at it, louder and louder. Notice how loudly you have to speak before it spins — if it does at all. This shows you how the airspeed for speaking is much slower than for breathing. Next, sing at the windmill. See how it starts turning at a lower volume than when you spoke at it.

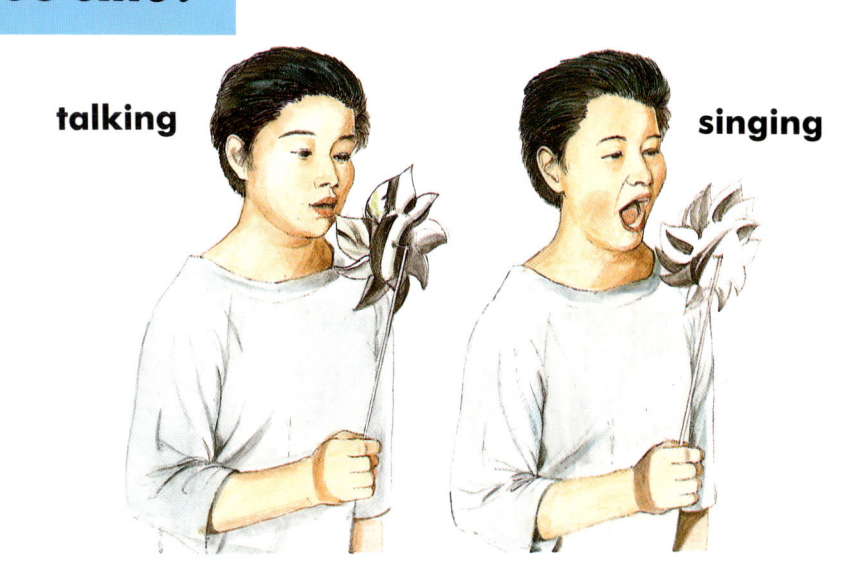

talking

singing

VOLUME FACTS

- Sounds measuring more than 90 dB can damage your hearing if they carry on for a long time.
- A pneumatic drill, 1 metre away, registers about 100 dB.
- The loudest sound made by a living creature is the deafening moaning grunt of a blue whale. It registers more than 180 dB.
- The eerie call of the humpback whale can be heard over 100 kilometres away through the ocean.
- In still air, the words of a person shouting can be heard 200 metres away.
- The whoops of the male South American howler monkey can be clearly heard over 1 kilometre away in the jungle.

Shaping sounds

The sounds made by your vocal cords are quite dull and quiet. If you heard these sounds on their own, you would hardly recognize them. Other parts of your neck and head give speech and singing their special sounds. These parts include the back of your throat, your tongue, teeth, cheeks, lips and sinuses. They work together to "shape" sounds and give your voice its unique character.

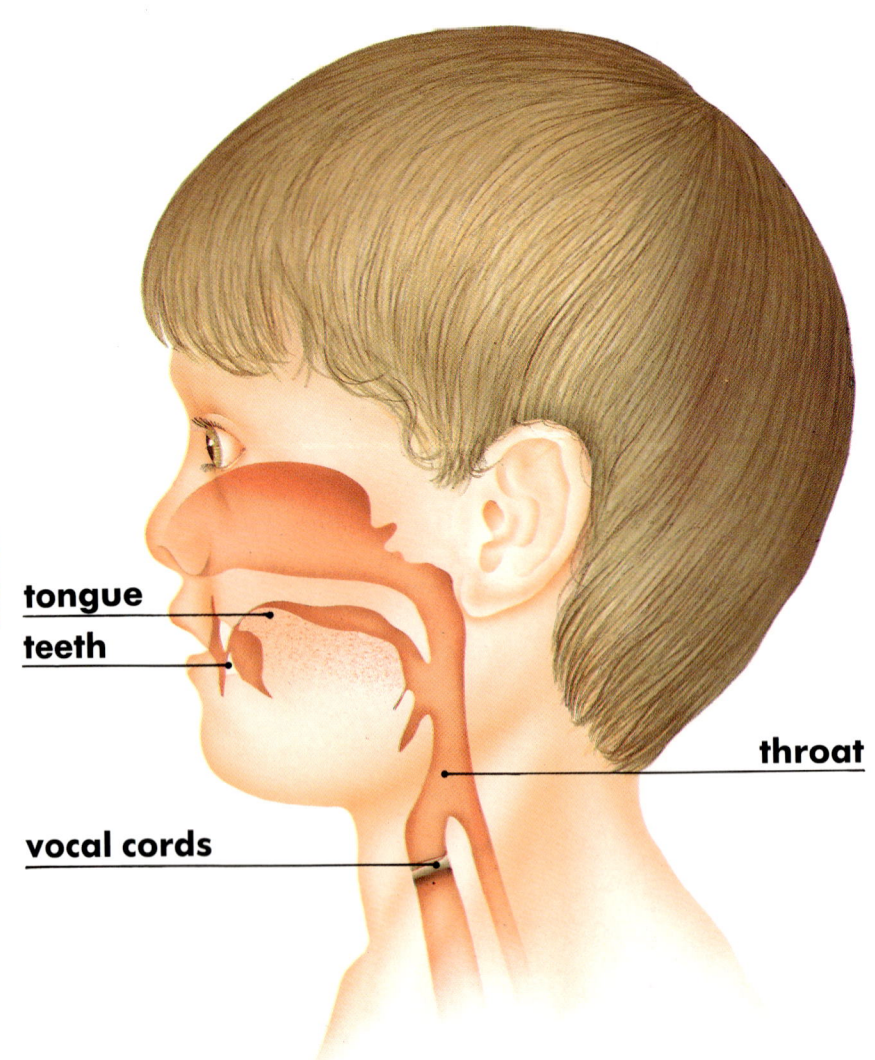

△ Watch how your lips change shape when you say "Eeee..."
▽ then "Oooo".

▷ Say "Goat, Kite, Train". Hear how the "G" sound starts in your throat, the "K" at the back of the roof of your mouth, and the "T" in the front.

tongue
teeth
vocal cords
throat

THE SINUSES

There are several pairs of holes in your skull which are filled with air. They are called your sinuses. They are connected by openings and tubes to the main airways of your nose and mouth. The air in the sinuses vibrates when you speak or sing, and helps to make your voice louder and clearer. When you have a cold, your sinuses may become blocked with slimy mucus. This makes your voice sound different.

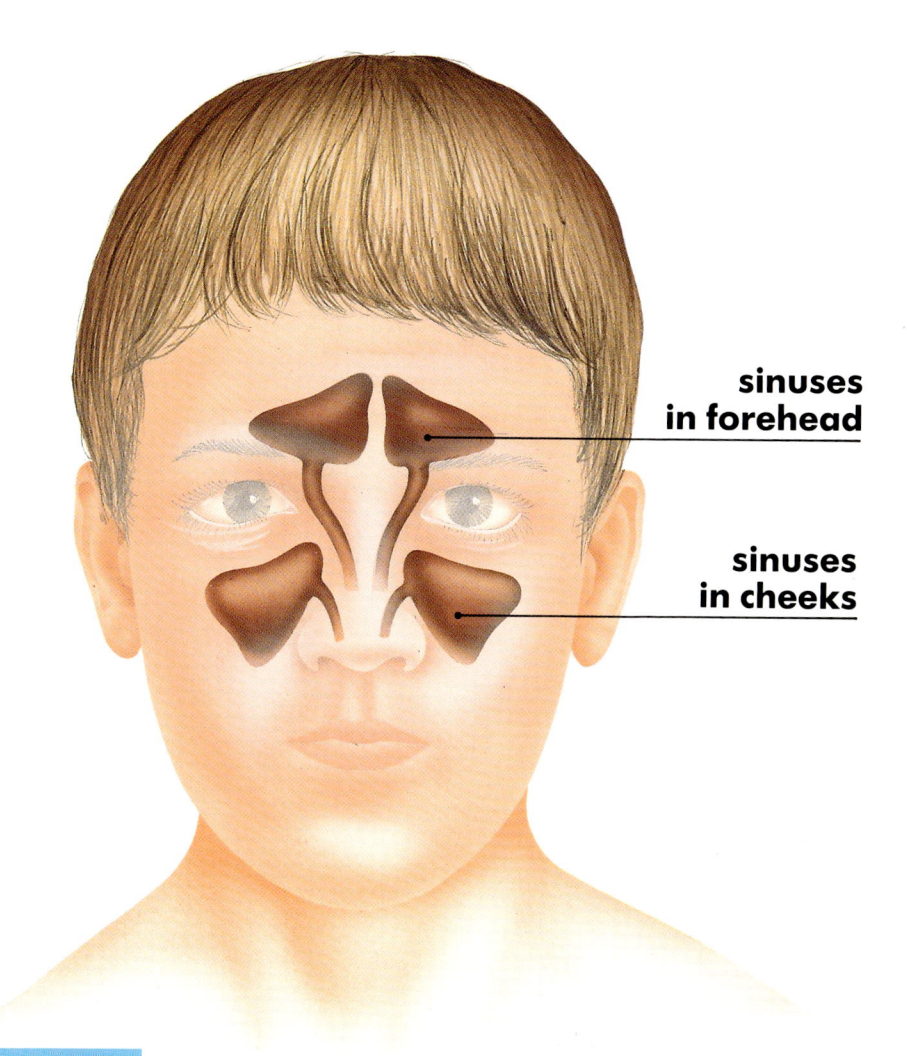

sinuses in forehead

sinuses in cheeks

SINGING A STRANGE SONG

You can hear how important each part of your speech-making system is, by changing different parts as you sing. Try keeping your lips still as you shape the words. Then try not to move your tongue. You could try holding your nose and singing as shown here, to hear the effect of shutting off your nasal cavity and upper sinuses. Can you say "nose" while you do this? Does it sound more like "doze?" Now let go of your nose and put a piece of bread over your teeth to partly block the airflow.

SHAPE AND SOUND FACTS

- When an object and any air in it vibrate, they produce sound — just like your vocal cords and your head.
- Many musical instruments contain air. They have special shapes to help them produce clear, musical notes.
- When you cover the different holes of a recorder with your fingers, you alter the amount of vibrating air inside the instrument. This changes the pitch of the notes you play.
- Pressing the valves on a trumpet, or moving the slide of a trombone also changes the amount of air inside it.
- In general, bigger objects that contain more air vibrate at lower frequencies. Because of this, they emphasize low-pitched notes (see page 24).

CAN YOU SEE SPEECH?

As you sing or speak, people can hear the sounds you make. They may also watch how your face and lips move. To find out how seeing helps you understand speech, blindfold a friend and whisper a short sentence in his or her ear. Then repeat the sentence with the blindfold off. Your friend should find it much easier to pick out the words if he or she can see your lips as well as hear the words. People who have hearing problems often rely on "lip-reading" to help them work out what is being said.

Singing and speaking

Your voicebox cannot talk or sing on its own. Its muscles are controlled by nerves that link it to your brain. When you want to sing, tiny nerve signals flash from your brain, along the nerves, to the muscles in your voicebox and neck, throat, mouth, tongue, cheeks and lips. Singing relies on all these muscles working together.

△ If you are nervous, you may get "stage fright" and forget the words to your song. Your brain is so busy worrying that it forgets to tell your voicebox what to say.

▷ The "thinking" part of your brain is called the cerebral cortex. Nerves run from it to the dozens of muscles in your face and neck, which are concerned with singing.

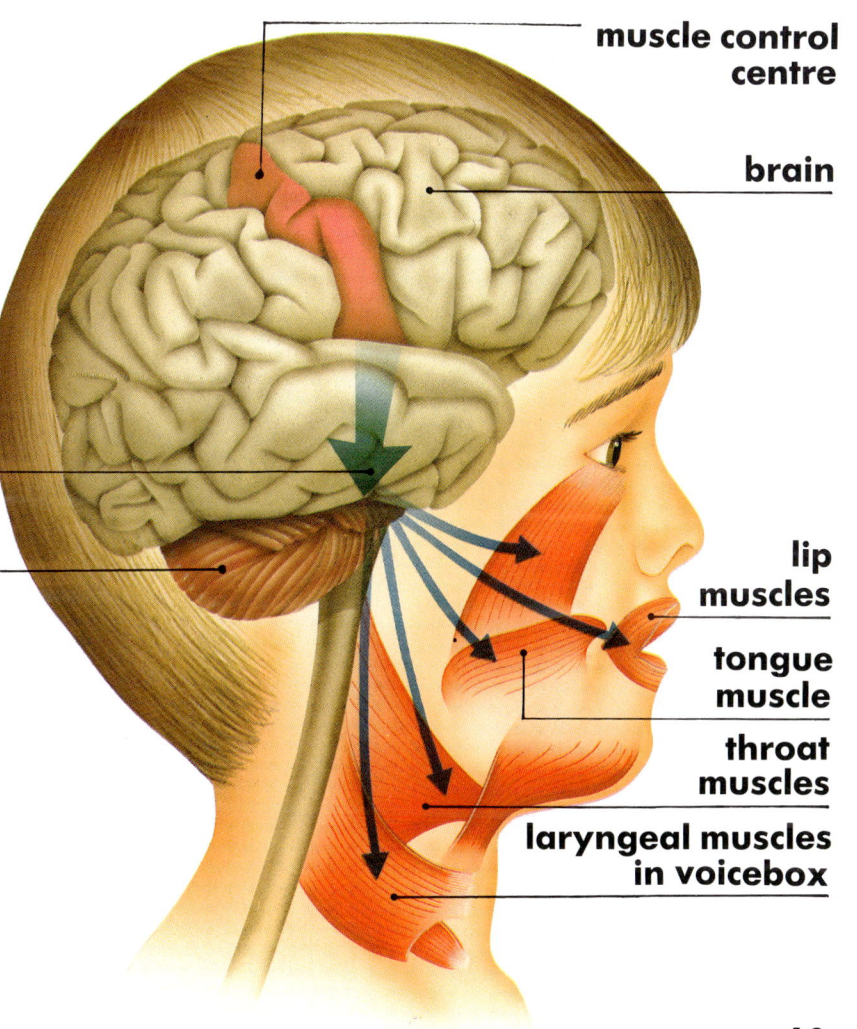

muscle control centre
brain
nerve signals
cerebral cortex of brain
lip muscles
tongue muscle
throat muscles
laryngeal muscles in voicebox

CHOOSING YOUR WORDS

1 First you see something.

2 Get the idea of what you want to say.

3 Choose the most important main words.

4 Make them into a sentence. Brain sends the correct nerve signals to the muscles of your speech system.

5 The voicebox and other parts work together to make the sounds come out of your mouth.

CAR

careful car

"Be careful, here comes a car."

The processes of speaking or singing are much more complicated than they at first seem. This is especially true if you are making up what you say, rather than reading something already written. A great deal has to happen in your brain, before the nerve signals can travel out to the muscles of your head and neck.

SPEECH FACTS

- The complex processes of learning to talk and sing can sometimes go wrong.
- Some people know what they want to say, but cannot say it clearly. They stumble over words or have to repeat the first part of a word several times. These speech defects are called stammering or stuttering.
- Nowadays, experts known as speech therapists can help many people with speech defects. They use many different types of equipment, such as videotapes and computers.

THE SPEECH CENTRE

The part of your brain which controls talking, singing and other sounds is called the speech centre. It works closely with the hearing centre which understands words spoken to you, the vision centre which deals with written words and what you see, and the control centre which controls your movements. These centres work together when you perform complicated movements, such as reading out loud what you are writing down, or singing as you conduct.

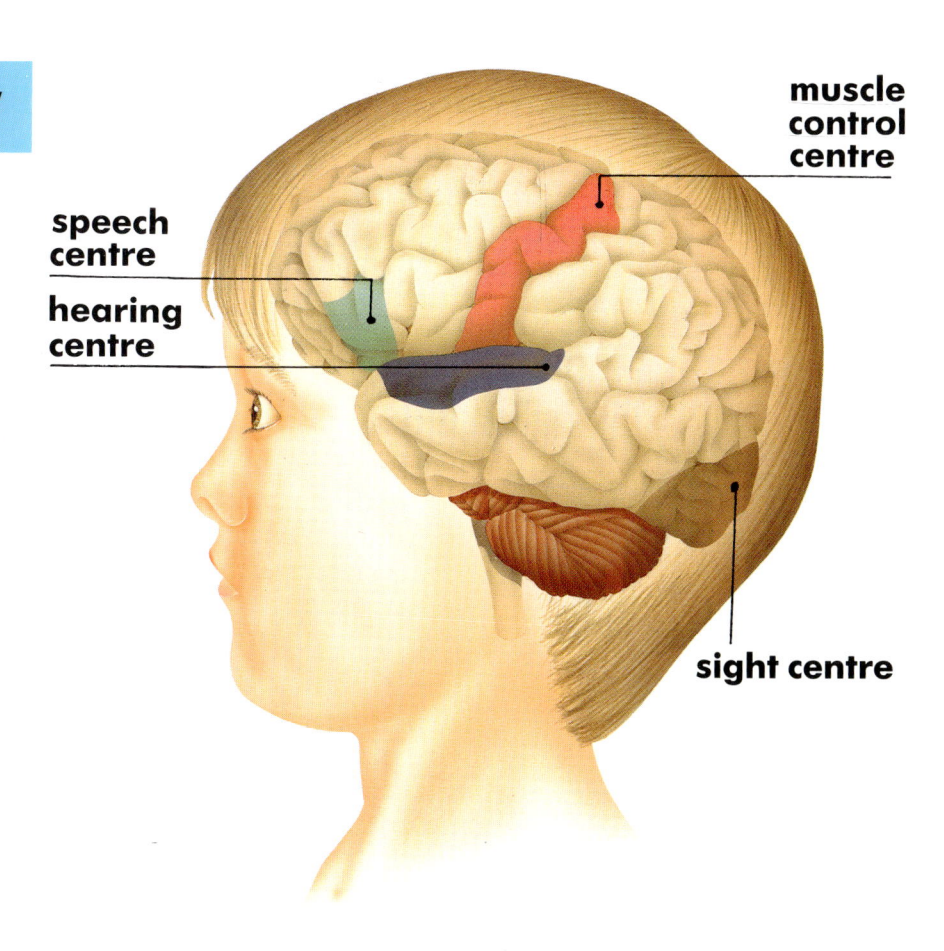

CAN YOU MAKE UP A TUNE?

The rhythm of a song, its volume and the expression you put into it, are sometimes more important than the words themselves. Try swapping tunes and singing styles around. For example, sing a quiet lullaby as though you were a parent lulling your baby to sleep. Now sing the same words but imagine you are a rock star, performing in front of thousands of fans. Make up a suitable tune, on the spot. Try other styles, such as pop, rap and opera.

Blowing, coughing, sneezing

Your mouth, nose, throat, voicebox, windpipe and lungs form your respiratory system. Their main job is to make you breathe, or respire. Speech and singing are extra features of this system. You also use this system when you blow, cough and sneeze. The last two actions are part of your body's natural defences. They help you to get rid of excess mucus, or dust you might have breathed in.

△ Learning the correct way to blow makes playing the trumpet much easier. When you blow through pursed lips, the air flows through a narrow hole. It rushes out much more forcefully than if your mouth was open wide. Your abdominal muscles push the air out of your lungs.

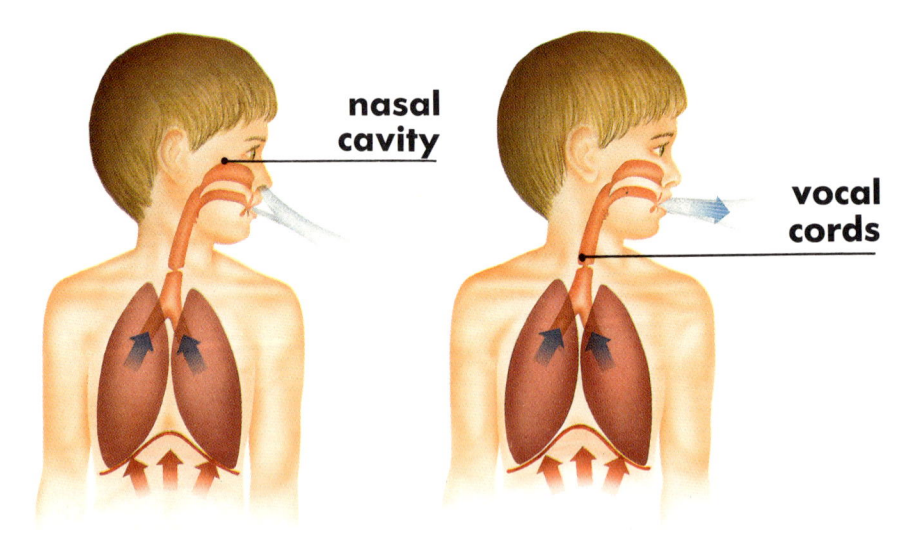

△ Before you sneeze, you close the back of your nasal cavity and the top of your throat as the pressure builds up in your lungs. Then, you open the airway and the air hurtles out of your nose.

△ For a cough, your larynx closes as your abdominal muscles increase the pressure in your lungs. When you open your larynx, the air rushes out, rattling your vocal cords.

HOW FAST CAN YOU BLOW?

An anemometer is a device that measures wind-speed. Try making your own anemometer to measure how fast you can blow. Glue together two thin strips of wood and four yogurt pots, as shown on the right. Glue this on to an old ballpoint pen. Stick a cotton reel in the base of a shoe box, and make a hole through the shoe box lid. Stand the pen in the cotton reel. Blow at the anemometer, then time how long it takes to stop spinning. Ask your friends to have a go. Now try with a hair-dryer or fan and compare the results.

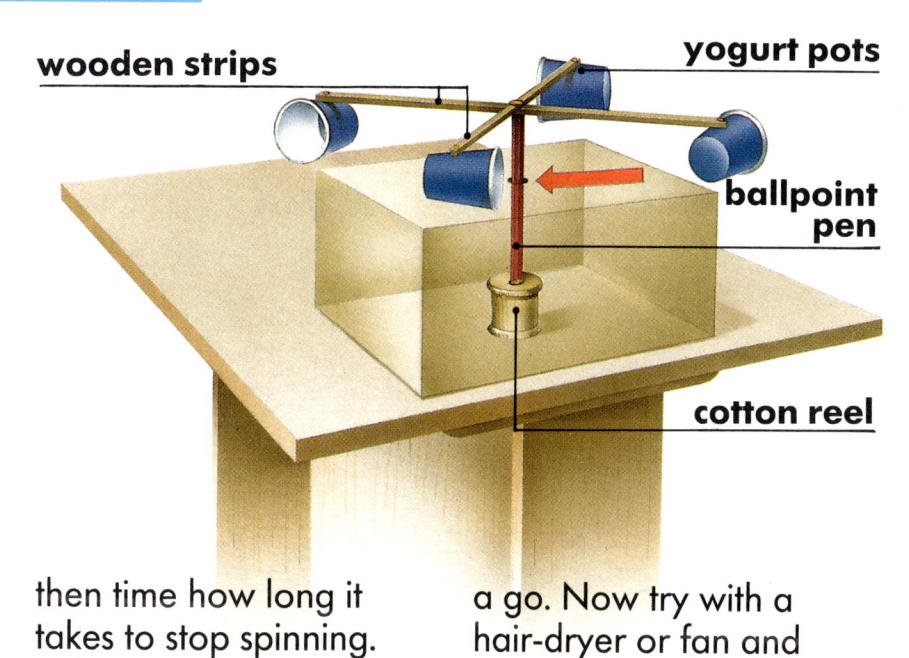

wooden strips — **yogurt pots** — **ballpoint pen** — **cotton reel**

HOW FAR CAN YOU BLOW?

To test how far you can blow, try a game of blow-skittles. Cut the skittle shapes out of stiff card. Fold the bases of the skittles towards you so they will stand up. Now blow at the skittles from different distances, starting at about an arm's length away. How far away are you when you cannot blow the skittles over any more? Get your friends to have a go, and compare their results to yours. You could also try blowing at the skittles through various objects to see if they help. Try a wide drinking straw, or a plastic household funnel. Blow through the wide end first, then through the narrow end.

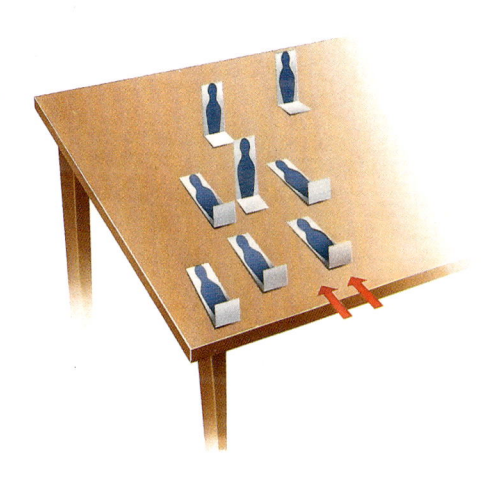

Changing voices

As you grow up, your respiratory system gets bigger. As we saw on page 18, bigger objects, which contain more air, usually vibrate at lower frequencies. This means that an adult's voice is usually lower-pitched than a baby's voice. Your own voice gets deeper as your body grows. If you are a boy, it will become much deeper when you are a teenager. This is when your voice "breaks". It happens as your vocal cords become thicker.

△ An adult man has thicker vocal cords than you have, and can sing much deeper. But can he sing as high as you can?

▷ In an orchestra, each group of instruments plays a wide range of notes, from very low to very high.

tuba **cornet** **double-bass** **violin** **bassoon** **piccolo**

In the brass section, the huge tuba makes a deep "oom-pah" sound. The smaller cornet works in the same way but its notes are much higher.

In the string section, the double-bass makes very deep sounds. The violin is a similar shape but smaller. It makes much higher sounds.

In the woodwind section, the bassoon is a vibrating tube that makes rich, deep notes. The tiny piccolo makes notes many times higher.

MAKING HIGH AND LOW SOUNDS

This simple project demonstrates how bigger objects or those containing more air usually vibrate at lower frequencies. Half fill a clean glass bottle with water. Tap the bottle with a spoon, or blow across the top to make a hooting sound. Remember the pitch of the note. Now tip some of the water out, and tap or blow again. Has the pitch (frequency) of the sound gone up or down? Tip out some more water, and try again. As the air space inside the bottle gets bigger, the pitch of the sound it makes gets lower. Use several bottles to make a simple musical instrument like the xylophone on page 29.

deeper note

higher note

VOICE FACTS

- A full choir has several groups of singers. Each group sings a different range of notes.
- Choral music is written so that the different notes blend together, into a pleasing overall sound.
- The lowest notes are sung by the bass section. They are men, who stand at the back of the choir.
- Tenors sing the next range of notes up. They are men with higher voices than basses.
- Next come the altos, who sing higher notes than tenors. They can be men or women.
- Sopranos sing the highest notes of all. They are usually adult women with high-pitched voices, or young boys (called trebles) or girls.

25

Caring for your voice

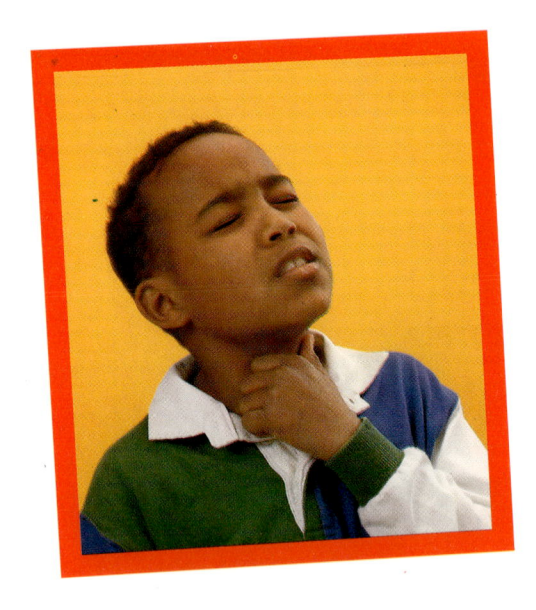

If you tried to run a long race without training beforehand, you would soon give up as your muscles got tired and your joints became sore. If you tried to use your voice too much without proper training and practice, the same thing would happen. Your vocal cords, especially, would become red, swollen, sore and painful. The muscles in your larynx and neck might also get strained. So it is important to train your voice, and to take time to practise your singing.

△ Using your voice for too long, or shouting, can damage your speech system. Your voice becomes weak, and croaky, or hoarse.

▷ Various people use their voice a lot, as part of their job. They include teachers, auctioneers, radio disc jockeys, and singers. Other people may shout or scream themselves hoarse now and again, such as fans at a sports event.

VOICE CARE FACTS

- Avoid suddenly using your voice a lot. Work up to it gradually, after practising for a few days. People who use their voices a lot often have microphones, so they can be heard clearly without straining their voices.
- If you want to learn to sing well, ask a singing teacher for advice. He or she will teach you how to breathe correctly and how to sing without straining your voice.
- Before you sing, do some warm-up exercises with your voice — in the same way that an athlete warms up by doing stretching exercises before a race.
- Tobacco smoke can damage your voicebox, as well as having many other bad effects on your health.

CAN YOU MAKE YOURSELF HEARD?

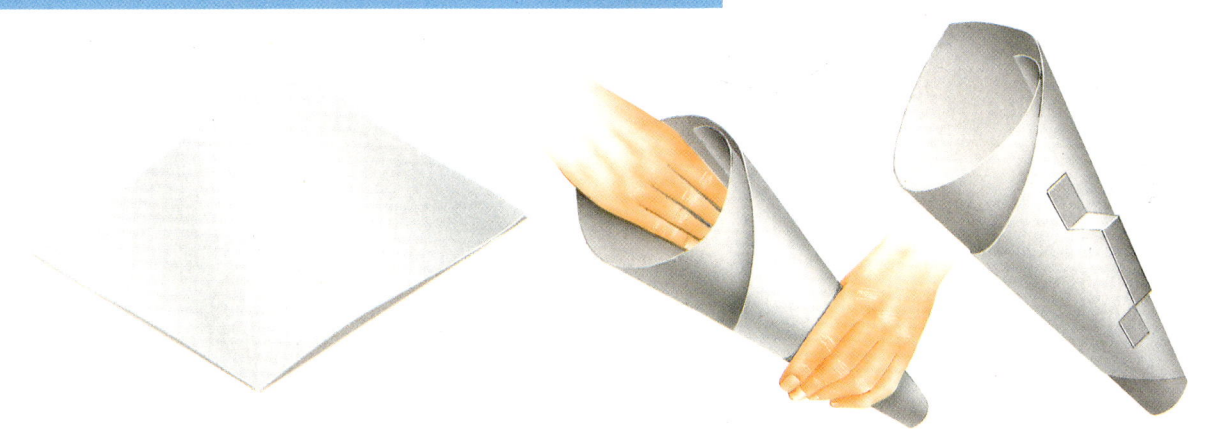

A megaphone helps you to be heard, without straining your voice. To make your own megaphone, cut out a large square of stiff card. Roll the card into a funnel shape and tape or glue it together. Make a handle from a strip of card and glue it to the megaphone, as shown. Stand a few metres away from a friend and talk to him or her first without the megaphone, then with it. How much difference does it make?

Things to do

GUESSING SOUNDS

Each human voice has a special character that we learn to recognize. This is made up of the actual sound of the voice, together with the way a person talks and pronounces words, how loud their voice is, and whether he or she has an accent. If you have a tape recorder, tape your family or friends — not only talking, but singing, and making noises such as laughing or crying, coughing and humming. Record each person separately. Play back the tape and ask them to guess who's who. Tape them again as they read a passage from a book while smiling, or grinning, or frowning. Can the others guess their facial expressions from the tape-recording and from the way the words are altered?

SPEECH SPEED

Most people find it difficult to speak clearly at over 300 words a minute. Try reading a book out loud to a friend, as quickly as you can. The friend should stop you if she or he cannot make out the words. Read for one minute, then count how many words you have said, to find out your speed per minute. Can you read out loud as fast as your friend can read silently to herself or himself? You could also tape-record a fast-talking gameshow host or a sports commentator and count the number of words they use.

LISTEN TO THE EXPERTS

Try listening to some recordings, of famous singers. Can you detect when they breathe in? Is it between the lines or phrases of the song? See if you can talk or sing while you are breathing in. It is almost impossible to do! What do you think makes a great singer? There are many aspects. Some are obvious, such as whether he or she can pronounce the words and sing in tune. What about the character of the voice, and whether she or he sings with "feeling"? What about the singer's appearance? Is it the song that makes a hit record, or the singer, or both?

SPEED AND VOLUME

Use the home-made anemometer on page 23 in some other experiments. Try whispering at the anemometer, talking quietly, speaking more loudly, shouting, singing, blowing and even sucking. You could blow with a bicycle pump, wave a hand-held fan, or go outside and test the wind on a gusty day. Reverse two of the cups on the anemometer, and try to blow it one way as much as the wind is blowing it the other way, to keep it still. Be careful not to blow too much or you may feel light-headed or dizzy.

THE HOME ORCHESTRA

Get together with friends to make some "musical instruments" from things around your home. You could stretch a balloon as it deflates, so that the screeching and squeezing sound rises or falls in pitch. (This is how your vocal cords work, see page 7.) A row of jam jars filled with different amounts of water, and tapped with a teaspoon, makes a simple xylophone. Adjust the amounts of water to produce a simple musical scale. Place your thumb over the end of a bicycle pump and push the other end, lifting your thumb slightly to make different squeaks and squeals as the air rushes out of the pump. Can you all play a simple song together?

29

Glossary

Alveoli Microscopic air bubbles in the lung. They are surrounded by tiny blood vessels, which absorb oxygen from the air in the alveoli. There are 300 million or more alveoli in each lung.

Brain A large, tangled "lump" of interconnected nerves inside the head. It is the control centre of the body. Other nerves link it to the various body parts.

Centre A part of the brain specialized to deal with nerve messages coming in from, or going out to, a certain part of the body. For example, the speech centre deals with messages in the form of words.

Cochlea A spiral-shaped part deep in the ear, involved in hearing. It turns vibrations into nerve signals and sends them to the brain.

Decibel (dB or dBA) A measure of the loudness or volume of a sound. A decibel actually measures the amplitude or "height" of the sound wave in the air.

Diaphragm A sheet of muscle at the base of the chest, that divides the chest from the abdomen. It is dome-shaped when relaxed, and flattens as it pulls or contracts when breathing in.

Frequency The number of complete sound waves per second passing through the air, or the number of vibrations per second of a solid object. The higher the frequency, the higher the pitch of a musical note. Frequencies are usually measured in Hertz (Hz).

Hertz A measurement of frequency. One Hertz (Hz) is one cycle per second. Most people can hear sounds of frequencies from about 30 to 12-15,000 Hz.

Larynx A box-like structure in the neck at the top of the windpipe, made of plates of cartilage and muscles. Sometimes called the voicebox, it contains the vocal cords.

Muscle Part of the body that can contract, or get shorter. As it does so it pulls on other parts, such as bones or other muscles, and moves them.

Nasal cavity The hole behind the nose, above the mouth. It opens into the throat at the back, the sinuses at the sides, and the nostrils at the front.

Nerve A long, thin bundle of neurones (nerve cells) that carries nerve messages from one part of the body to another.

Nerve message A series of tiny bursts of electricity that travel along a nerve, very much like electrical signals going along a telephone wire.

Pitch Whether a sound is high or low on the musical scale, depending on its frequency.

Vocal cords Two whitish folds of the larynx wall, that vibrate to produce the sounds used in speech and singing.

Resources

ORGANIZATIONS

Health Education Authority
78 New Oxford Street, London WC1A 1AH
Provides leaflets and information on many aspects of health and fitness

BOOKS

Your Body by Steve Parker
Piccolo Factbooks, Piper Books, London
A small pocket-book introduction to the workings of the human body

The Human Body by Linda Gamlin
Today's World Series, Watts/Gloucester
A system-by-system account of the body and how it works

The Human Body – New Edition by Steve Parker
An 8-volume series, Watts, London
Each volume covers one main part or system of the body, such as the Brain and Nerves, or the Ear and Hearing

The Human Body – Your Body and How It Works by Ruth and Bertel Bruun
Kingfisher Library of Knowledge
A fully illustrated look at the body, from microscopic cells to whole organs, and how they work together

The Body and How It Works by Steve Parker
Windows on the World series, Dorling Kindersley, London
An imaginary journey around each region of the body, from the head and neck to the feet and toes

The Human Body and The Facts of Life by Jonathan Miller and David Pelham
Jonathan Cape Limited, London
Pop-up books with moving flaps, levers to pull, and working parts

Index

abdomen 22, 30
air pressure 7, 9
airspeed 15
alveoli 9, 30
amplitude 30
anemometer 23, 29

bassoon 24
bats 12
blood 8
blood vessels 30
bones 13, 31
brain 13, 19, 20, 21, 30
breathing 6, 8-10, 14, 15, 22, 27, 30
bronchi 9

carbon dioxide 8
cartilage 6, 31
centre 21, 30
cerebral cortex 19
cheeks 16, 17, 19
chest 8, 9, 11, 30
choir 25
cochlea 13, 30
coughing 22, 28

decibels 7, 15, 30
diaphragm 4, 8, 9, 14, 30
dolphins 12
double-bass 24

ears 12, 13, 30
electrical signals 13, 31
elephants 12

facial expressions 5, 28
frequency 11, 12, 13, 18, 24, 25, 30, 31

head 16, 18, 20, 30
hearing 15, 21
heart 8, 9
Hertz 11, 30
high pressure 7

infrasound 12
intercostal muscles 30

laryngeal muscles 19
larynx 4, 6, 12, 22, 26, 30-31
learning 20
lip-reading 18
lips 10, 16, 18, 19, 22
low pressure 7
lungs 4, 6, 8, 9, 10, 22, 30

megaphone 27
microphone 27
mouth 4, 6, 7, 17, 19, 20, 22, 31
mucus 17, 22
muscles 6, 11, 12, 19, 20, 22, 26, 30, 31
music 4, 25, 30
musical instruments 18, 24, 29

nasal cavity 4, 17, 22, 31
neck 4, 6, 11, 16, 19, 20, 26, 31
nerve signals 13, 19, 30
nerves 19, 20, 30, 31
neurones 31
nose 6, 17, 22, 31

orchestra 24
outer ear 13
oxygen 8, 9, 30

piccolo 24
pitch 11, 12, 13, 18, 24, 25, 29, 30, 31

recorder 18
respiratory system 22, 24
rhythm 21
ribs 4, 8, 14, 30

sinuses 16, 17, 31
skull 17
sneezing 22
sound waves 7, 11, 30
speech centre 21, 30
speech defects 20

throat 4, 6, 16, 19, 22, 31
tongue 4, 6, 10, 16, 17, 19
trumpet 18, 22

ultrasound 12

vibrations 6, 7, 11, 13, 17, 18, 24, 25, 30
violin 24
vision centre 21
vocal cords 6, 7, 8, 11, 12, 16, 18, 22, 24, 26, 29, 31
voice training 26
voicebox 4, 6, 8, 19, 20, 22, 31
volume 7

whales 15
whispering 7, 18, 29
whistling 10
wind-speed 23
windpipe 4, 6, 8, 22, 31

xylophone 25, 29, 31